Police and Criminal Evidence Act 1984 (PACE)

CODE E Revised

Code of Practice on audio recording interviews with suspects

CODE F Revised

Code of Practice on visual recording with sound of interviews with suspects

GRAN*GIS* UK Publishing

Adapted and Published by GRANGIS (Grand Register Library).
Online: www.grangis.com.
E-mail: contact@grangis.com.

© GRANGIS 2022.
In this version:
ISBN: 979-8-88559-093-8
Where we have identified any copyrighted material, you will need to obtain written permission for re-use.
Note: Title, sub-title and version of this publication is as described. For the most recent information please visit www.gov.uk.

© Crown copyright 2018

This information is licensed under the Open Government Licence v3.0. To view this licence:

visit   https://www.nationalarchives.gov.uk/doc/open-government-licence/version/3/
email   psi@nationalarchives.gsi.gov.uk

About this publication:

enquiries www.gov.uk/contactus
download www.gov.uk/government/publications

POLICE AND CRIMINAL EVIDENCE ACT 1984 (PACE)

CODE E

REVISED

CODE OF PRACTICE ON AUDIO RECORDING INTERVIEWS WITH SUSPECTS

Commencement - Transitional Arrangements

This Code applies to interviews carried out after 00.00 on 31 July 2018, notwithstanding that the interview may have commenced before that time.

Code E - Contents

1 General

1.0 The procedures in this Code must be used fairly, responsibly, with respect for the people to whom they apply and without unlawful discrimination. Under the Equality Act 2010, section 149 (Public Sector Equality Duty), police forces must, in carrying out their functions, have due regard to the need to eliminate unlawful discrimination, harassment, victimisation and any other conduct which is prohibited by that Act, to advance equality of opportunity between people who share a relevant protected characteristic and people who do not share it, and to foster good relations between those persons. The Equality Act *also* makes it unlawful for police officers to discriminate against, harass or victimise any person on the grounds of the 'protected characteristics' of age, disability, gender reassignment, race, religion or belief, sex and sexual orientation, marriage and civil partnership, pregnancy and maternity, when using their powers. See *Note 1B*.

1.1 This Code of Practice must be readily available for consultation by:

- police officers
- police staff
- detained persons
- members of the public.

1.2 The *Notes for Guidance* included are not provisions of this Code. They form guidance to police officers and others about its application and interpretation.

1.3 Nothing in this Code shall detract from the requirements of Code C, the Code of Practice for the detention, treatment and questioning of persons by police officers.

1.4 The interviews and other matters to which this Code applies are described in section 2. This Code does not apply to the conduct and recording in England and Wales, of:

- interviews of persons detained under section 41 of, or Schedule 7 to, the Terrorism Act 2000, and
- post-charge questioning of persons authorised under section 22 of the Counter-Terrorism Act 2008.

These must be video recorded with sound in accordance with the provisions of the separate Code of Practice issued under *paragraph 3 of Schedule 8 to the Terrorism Act 2000* and under *section 25 of the Counter-Terrorism Act 2008*. If, during the course of an interview or questioning under this Code, it becomes apparent that the interview or questioning should be conducted under that separate Code, the interview should only continue in accordance with that Code.

Note: The provisions of this Code and Code F which govern the conduct and recording of interviews *do not apply* to interviews with, or taking statements from, witnesses.

1.5 In this Code:

- 'appropriate adult' has the same meaning as in Code C, *paragraph 1.7.*
- 'vulnerable person' has the same meaning as described in Code C *paragraph 1.13(d).*
- 'solicitor' has the same meaning as in Code C, *paragraph 6.12.*
- 'interview' has the same meaning as in *Code C, paragraph 11.1A.*

1.5A The provisions of this Code which require interviews with suspects to be audio recorded and the provisions of Code F which permit simultaneous visual recording provide safeguards:

- for suspects against inaccurate recording of the words used in questioning them and of their demeanour during the interview; and;
- for police interviewers against unfounded allegations made by, or on behalf of, suspects about the conduct of the interview and what took place during the interview which might otherwise appear credible.

Recording of interviews must therefore be carried out openly to instil confidence in its reliability as an impartial and accurate record of the interview.

1.5B The provisions of Code C:

- *sections 10 and 11*, and the applicable *Notes for Guidance* apply to the conduct of interviews to which this Code applies.
- *paragraphs 11.7 to 11.14* apply only when a written record is needed.

1.5C Code C, *paragraphs 10.10, 10.11* and *Annex C* describe the restriction on drawing adverse inferences from an arrested suspect's failure or refusal to say anything about their involvement in the offence when interviewed or after being charged or informed they may be prosecuted, and how it affects the terms of the caution and determines if and by whom a special warning under sections 36 and 37 of the Criminal Justice and Public Order Act 1994 can be given.

1.6 In this Code:

(a) in relation to the place where an interview of a suspect to which this Code or (as the case may be) Code F, applies, is conducted and recorded (see *Note 1A*):

   (i) '*authorised*' in relation to the recording devices described in (ii) and (iii), means any such device that the chief officer has authorised interviewers under their direction and control to use to record the interview in question at the place in question, provided that the interviewer in question has been trained to set up and operate the device, in compliance with the manufacturer's instructions and subject to the operating procedures required by the chief officer;

   (ii) '*removable recording media device*' means a recording device which, when set up and operated in accordance with the manufacturer's instructions and the operating procedures required by the chief officers, uses removable, physical recording media (such as magnetic tape, optical disc or solid state memory card) for the purpose of making a clear and accurate, audio recording or (as the case may be) audio-visual recording, of the interview in question which can then be played back and copied using that device or any other device. A sign or indicator on the device which is visible to the suspect must show when the device is recording;

   (iii) '*secure digital recording network device*' means a recording device which, when set up and operated in accordance with the manufacturer's instructions and the operating procedures required by the chief officers, enables a clear and accurate original audio recording or (as the case may be) audio-visual recording, of the interview in question, to be made and stored using non-removable storage, as a digital file or a series of such files that can be securely transferred by a wired or wireless connection to a remote secure network file server system (which may have cloud based storage) which ensures that access to interview recordings for all purposes is strictly controlled and is restricted to those whose access, either generally or in specific cases, is necessary. Examples of access include playing back the whole or part of any original recording and making one or more copies of, the whole or part of that original recording. A sign or indicator on the device which is visible to the suspect must show when the device is recording.

(b) 'designated person' means a person other than a police officer, who has specified powers and duties conferred or imposed on them by designation under section 38 or 39 of the Police Reform Act 2002.

(c) any reference to a police officer includes a designated person acting in the exercise or performance of the powers and duties conferred or imposed on them by their designation.

1.7 Section 2 of this Code sets out the requirement that an authorised recording device, if available, must be used to record a suspect interview and when such a device cannot be used, it allows a 'relevant officer' (see *paragraph 2.3(c)*) to decide that the interview is to be recorded in writing in accordance with Code C. For detained suspects, the 'relevant officer' is the custody officer and for voluntary interviews, the officer is determined according to the type of offence (indictable or summary only) and where the interview takes place (police station or elsewhere). Provisions in sections 3 and 4 deal with the conduct and recording of interviews according to the type of authorised recording device used. Section 3 applies to *removable recording media devices* (see *paragraph 1.6(a)(i)*) and section 4 applies to *secure digital recording network devices* (see *paragraph 1.6(a)(ii)*). The Annex applies when a voluntary interview is conducted elsewhere than at a police station about one of the four offence types specified in the Annex. For such interviews, the relevant officer is the interviewer.

1.8   Nothing in this Code prevents the custody officer, or other officer given custody of the detainee, from allowing police staff who are not designated persons to carry out individual procedures or tasks at the police station if the law allows. However, the officer remains responsible for making sure the procedures and tasks are carried out correctly in accordance with this Code. Any such police staff must be:

(a) a person employed by a police force and under the control and direction of the Chief Officer of that force; or

(b) employed by a person with whom a police force has a contract for the provision of services relating to persons arrested or otherwise in custody.

1.9   Designated persons and other police staff must have regard to any relevant provisions of the Codes of Practice.

1.10   References to pocket book shall include any official report book or electronic recording device issued to police officers or police staff that enables a record required to be made by any provision of this Code (but which is not an audio record to which *paragraph 2.1* applies) to be made and dealt with in accordance with that provision. References in this Code to written records, forms and signatures include electronic records and forms and electronic confirmation that identifies the person making the record or completing the form.

Chief officers must be satisfied as to the integrity and security of the devices, records and forms to which this paragraph applies and that use of those devices, records and forms satisfies relevant data protection legislation.

1.11   References to a custody officer include those performing the functions of a custody officer as in *paragraph 1.9* of Code C.

1.12   *Not used.*

1.13   Nothing in this Code requires the identity of officers or police staff conducting interviews to be recorded or disclosed if the interviewer reasonably believes recording or disclosing their name might put them in danger. In these cases, the officers and staff should use warrant or other identification numbers and the name of their police station. Such instances and the reasons for them shall be recorded in the custody record or the interviewer's pocket book. (See *Note 1C*.)

Notes for Guidance

1A   *An interviewer who is not sure, or has any doubt, about whether a place or location elsewhere than a police station is suitable for carrying out an interview of a juvenile or vulnerable person, using a particular recording device, should consult an officer of the rank of sergeant or above for advice. See Code C paragraphs 3.21, 3.22 and Note 3I*

1B   *In paragraph 1.0, under the Equality Act 2010, section 149, the 'relevant protected characteristics' are: age, disability, gender reassignment, pregnancy and maternity, race, religion/belief, and sex and sexual orientation. For further detailed guidance and advice on the Equality Act, see: https://www.gov.uk/guidance/equality-act-2010-guidance.*

1C   *The purpose of paragraph 1.13 is to protect those involved in serious organised crime investigations or arrests of particularly violent suspects when there is reliable information that those arrested or their associates may threaten or cause harm to those involved. In cases of doubt, an officer of the rank of inspector or above should be consulted.*

1D *Attention is drawn to the provisions set out in Code C about the matters to be considered when deciding whether a detained person is fit to be interviewed.*

2 Interviews and other matters to be audio recorded under this Code

(A) Requirement to use authorised audio-recording device when available.

2.1 Subject to *paragraph 2.3*, if an authorised recording device (see *paragraph 1.6(a)*) in working order *and* an interview room or other location (see *Note 1A*) suitable for that device to be used, are available, then that device shall be used to record the following matters:

(a) any interview with a person cautioned in accordance with Code C, *section 10* in respect of any *summary* offence or any *indictable* offence, which includes any offence triable either way, when:

(i) that person (the suspect) is questioned about their involvement or suspected involvement in that offence and they have not been charged or informed they may be prosecuted for that offence; and

(ii) exceptionally, further questions are put to a person about any offence *after* they have been charged with, or told they may be prosecuted for, that offence (see Code C, *paragraph 16.5 and Note 2C*).

(b) when a person who has been charged with, or informed they may be prosecuted for, any offence, is told about any written statement or interview with another person and they are handed a true copy of the written statement or the content of the interview record is brought to their attention in accordance with Code C, *paragraph 16.4 and Note 2D*.

See *Note 2A*

2.2 The whole of each of the matters described in *paragraph 2.1* shall be audio-recorded, including the taking and reading back of any statement as applicable.

2.3 A written record of the matters described in *paragraph 2.1(a)* and *(b)* shall be made in accordance with Code C, *section 11*, only if,

(a) an authorised recording device (see *paragraph 1.6(a)*) in working order is *not available;* or

(b) such a device is available but a location suitable for using that device to make the audio recording of the matter in question is not available; and

(c) the 'relevant officer' described in *paragraph 2.4* considers on reasonable grounds, that the proposed interview or (as the case may be) continuation of the interview or other action, should not be delayed until an authorised recording device in working order *and* a suitable interview room or other location become available (see *Note 2E*) and decides that a written record shall be made;

(d) if in accordance with *paragraph 3.9*, the suspect or the appropriate adult on their behalf, objects to the interview being audibly recorded and the 'relevant officer' described in *paragraph 2.4*, after having regard to the nature and circumstances of the objections (see *Note 2F*), decides that a written record shall be made;

(e) in the case of a detainee who refuses to go into or remain in a suitable interview room and in accordance with Code C *paragraphs 12.5* and *12.11*, the custody officer directs that interview be conducted in a cell and considers that an authorised recording device cannot be safely used in the cell.

Note: When the suspect appears to have a hearing impediment, this paragraph does not affect the separate requirement in *paragraphs 3.7* and *4.4* for the interviewer to make a written note of the interview at the same time as the audio recording.

(B)   Meaning of 'relevant officer'

2.4   In *paragraph 2.3(c)*:

(a) if the person to be interviewed is arrested elsewhere than at a police station for an offence and before they arrive at a police station, an urgent interview in accordance with *Code C paragraph 11.1* is necessary to avert one or more of the risks mentioned in *sub-paragraphs (a)* to *(c)* of that paragraph, the 'relevant officer' means the *interviewer*, who may or may not be the arresting officer, who must have regard to the time, place and urgency of the proposed interview.

(b) if the person in question has been taken to a police station after being arrested elsewhere for an offence or is arrested for an offence whilst at a police station after attending voluntarily and is detained at that police station or elsewhere in the charge of a constable, the 'relevant officer' means the *custody officer at the station where the person's detention* was last authorised. The custody officer must have regard to the nature of the investigation and in accordance with *Code C paragraph 1.1*, ensure that the detainee is dealt with expeditiously, and released as soon as the need for their detention no longer applies.

(c) In the case of a voluntary interview (see *Code C paragraph 3.21* to *3.22*) which takes place:

(i) at a police station and the offence in question is an indictable offence, the 'relevant officer' means *an officer of the rank of sergeant or above*, in consultation with the investigating officer;

(ii) at a police station and the offence in question is a summary offence, the 'relevant officer' means *the interviewer* in consultation with the investigating officer if different,

(iii) elsewhere than at a police station and the offence is one of the four indictable offence types which satisfy the conditions in Part 1 of the <u>Annex</u> to this Code, the 'relevant officer' means *the interviewer* in consultation with the investigating officer, if different.

(iv) elsewhere than at a police station and the offence in question is an indictable offence which is not one of the four indictable offence types which satisfy the conditions in Part 1 of the <u>Annex</u> to this Code, the 'relevant officer' means an *officer of the rank of sergeant or above*, in consultation with the investigating officer.

(v) elsewhere than at a police station and the offence in question is a summary only offence, the 'relevant officer' means *the interviewer* in consultation with the investigating officer, if different.

See *<u>Note 2B –Summary table – relevant officer for voluntary interviews</u>*

(C)   Duties of the 'relevant officer' and the interviewer

2.5   When, in accordance with <u>*paragraph 2.3*</u>, a written record is made:

(a) the relevant officer must:

(i) record the reasons for not making an audio recording and the date and time the decision in <u>*paragraph 2.3(c)*</u> or (as applicable) <u>*paragraph 2.3(d)*</u> was made; and

(ii) ensure that the suspect is informed that a written record will be made;

(b) the interviewer must ensure that the written record includes:

(i) the date and time the decision in <u>*paragraph 2.3(c)*</u> or (as applicable) <u>*paragraph 2.3(d)*</u> was made, who made it and where the decision is recorded, and

(ii) the fact that the suspect was informed.

(c) the written record shall be made in accordance with Code C, *section 11*;

See *Note 2B*

(D) Remote monitoring of interviews

2.6 If the interview room or other location where the interview takes place is equipped with facilities that enable audio recorded interviews to be remotely monitored as they take place, the interviewer must ensure that suspects, their legal representatives and any appropriate adults are fully aware of what this means and that there is no possibility of privileged conversations being listened to. With this in mind, the following safeguards should be applied:

(a) The remote monitoring system should only be able to operate when the audio recording device has been turned on.

(b) The equipment should incorporate a light, clearly visible to all in the interview room, which is automatically illuminated as soon as remote monitoring is activated.

(c) Interview rooms and other locations fitted with remote monitoring equipment must contain a notice, prominently displayed, referring to the capacity for remote monitoring and to the fact that the warning light will illuminate whenever monitoring is taking place.

(d) At the beginning of the interview, the interviewer must explain the contents of the notice to the suspect and if present, to the solicitor and appropriate adult and that explanation should itself be audio recorded.

(e) The fact that an interview, or part of an interview, was remotely monitored should be recorded in the suspect's custody record or, if the suspect is not in detention, the interviewer's pocket book. That record should include the names of the officers doing the monitoring and the purpose of the monitoring (e.g. for training, to assist with the investigation, etc.)

(E) Use of live link - Interviewer not present at the same station as the detainee

2.7 Code C *paragraphs 12.9A* and *12.9B* set out the conditions which, if satisfied allow a suspect in police detention to be interviewed using a live link by a police officer who is not present at the police station where the detainee is held. These provisions also set out the duties and responsibilities of the custody officer, the officer having physical custody of the suspect and the interviewer and the modifications that apply to ensure that any such interview is conducted and audio recorded in accordance with this Code or (as the case may be) visually recorded in accordance with Code F.

Notes for Guidance

2A *Nothing in this Code is intended to preclude audio-recording at police discretion at police stations or elsewhere when persons are charged with, or told they may be prosecuted for, an offence or they respond after being so charged or informed.*

2B *A decision made in accordance with paragraph 2.3 not to audio-record an interview for any reason may be the subject of comment in court. The 'relevant officer' responsible should be prepared to justify that decision.*

Table: Summary of paragraph 2.4(c) – relevant officer for voluntary interviews:

	Location of voluntary interview	Offence type	Relevant Officer
(i)	Police station	Any indictable offence.	Sergeant or above[+]
(ii)	Police station	Any summary only offence	Interviewer[+]
(iii)	Elsewhere than at a police station	Indictable offence type defined by the Annex.	Interviewer[+]
(iv)	Elsewhere than at a police station	Indictable offence type not defined by the Annex.	Sergeant or above[+]
(v)	Elsewhere than at a police station	Summary only.	Interviewer[+]

[+] *= in consultation with the investigating officer.*

2C   *Code C sets out the circumstances in which a suspect may be questioned about an offence after being charged with it.*

2D   *Code C sets out the procedures to be followed when a person's attention is drawn after charge, to a statement made by another person. One method of bringing the content of an interview with another person to the notice of a suspect may be to play them a recording of that interview. The person may not be questioned about the statement or interview record unless this is allowed in accordance with paragraph 16.5 of Code C.*

2E   *A voluntary interview should be arranged for a time and place when it can be audio recorded and enable the safeguards and requirements set out in Code C paragraphs 3.21 to 3.22B to be implemented. It would normally be reasonable to delay the interview to enable audio recording unless the delay to do so would be likely to compromise the outcome of the interview or investigation, for example if there are grounds to suspect that the suspect would use the delay to fabricate an innocent explanation, influence witnesses or tamper with other material evidence.*

2F   *Objections for the purpose of paragraphs 2.3(d) and 3.9 are meant to apply to objections based on the suspect's genuine and honestly held beliefs and to allow officers to exercise their discretion to decide that a written interview record is to be made according to the circumstances surrounding the suspect and the investigation. Objections that appear to be frivolous with the intentions of frustrating or delaying the investigation would not be relevant.*

3   Interview recording using *removable recording media* device

(A) Recording and sealing master recordings - general

3.1   When using an authorised *removable recording media* device (see paragraph 1.6(a)(i)), one recording, the master recording, will be sealed in the suspect's presence. A second recording will be used as a working copy. The master recording is any of the recordings made by a multi-deck/drive machine or the only recording made by a single deck/drive machine. The working copy is one of the other recordings made by a multi-deck/drive machine or a copy of the master recording made by a single deck/drive machine.

3.2   The purpose of sealing the master recording before it leaves the suspect's presence is to establish their confidence that the integrity of the recording is preserved. If a single deck/drive machine is used the working copy of the master recording must be made in the suspect's presence and without the master recording leaving their sight. The working copy shall be used for making further copies if needed.

(B) Commencement of interviews

3.3   When the suspect is brought into the interview room or arrives at the location where the interview is to take place, the interviewer shall, without delay but in the suspect's sight, unwrap or open the new recording media, load the recording device with new recording media and set it to record.

3.4   The interviewer must point out the sign or indicator which shows that the recording equipment is activated and is recording (see paragraph 1.6(a)(i)) and shall then:

(a) tell the suspect that the interview is being audibly recorded using an authorised *removable recording media* device and outline the recording process (see Note 3A);

(b) subject to paragraph 1.13, give their name and rank and that of any other interviewer present;

(c) ask the suspect and any other party present, e.g. the appropriate adult, a solicitor or interpreter, to identify themselves (see Note 3A);

(d) state the date, time of commencement and place of the interview;

(e) tell the suspect that:

- they will be given a copy of the recording of the interview in the event that they are charged or informed that they will be prosecuted but if they are not charged or informed that they will be prosecuted they will only be given a copy as agreed with the police or on the order of a court; and

- they will be given a written notice at the end of the interview setting out their right to a copy of the recording and what will happen to the recording and;

(f) if equipment for remote monitoring of interviews as described in *paragraph 2.6* is installed, explain the contents of the notice to the suspect, solicitor and appropriate adult as required by *paragraph 2.6(d)* and point out the light that illuminates automatically as soon as remote monitoring is activated.

3.5 Any person entering the interview room after the interview has commenced shall be invited by the interviewer to identify themselves for the purpose of the audio recording and state the reason why they have entered the interview room.

3.6 The interviewer shall:

- caution the suspect, see Code C *section 10*; and
- if they are detained, remind them of their entitlement to free legal advice, see Code C, *paragraph 11.2*; or
- if they are not detained under arrest, explain this and their entitlement to free legal advice (see Code C, *paragraph 3.21*) and ask the suspect to confirm that they agree to the voluntary interview proceeding (see *Code C paragraph 3.22A*).

3.7 The interviewer shall put to the suspect any significant statement or silence, see Code C, *paragraph 11.4*.

(C) Interviews with suspects who appear to have a hearing impediment

3.8 If the suspect appears to have a hearing impediment, the interviewer shall make a written note of the interview in accordance with Code C, at the same time as audio recording it in accordance with this Code. (See *Notes 3B* and *3C*.)

(D) Objections and complaints by the suspect

3.9 If the suspect or an appropriate adult on their behalf, objects to the interview being audibly recorded either at the outset, during the interview or during a break, the interviewer shall explain that the interview is being audibly recorded and that this Code requires the objections to be recorded on the audio recording. When any objections have been audibly recorded or the suspect or appropriate adult have refused to have their objections recorded, the relevant officer shall decide in accordance with *paragraph 2.3(d)* (which requires the officer to have regard to the nature and circumstances of the objections) whether a written record of the interview or its continuation, is to be made and that audio recording should be turned off. Following a decision that a written record is to be made, the interviewer shall say they are turning off the recorder and shall then make a written record of the interview as in Code C, *section 11*. If, however, following a decision that a written record is not to be made, the interviewer may proceed to question the suspect with the audio recording still on. This procedure also applies in cases where the suspect has previously objected to the interview being visually recorded, see *Code F paragraph 2.7*, and the investigating officer has decided to audibly record the interview. (See *Notes 2F* and *3D*.)

3.10 If in the course of an interview a complaint is made by or on behalf of the person being questioned concerning the provisions of this or any other Codes, or it comes to the interviewer's notice that the person may have been treated improperly, the interviewer shall act as in Code C, *paragraph 12.9*. (See *Notes 3E* and *3F*.)

3.11 If the suspect indicates they want to tell the interviewer about matters not directly connected with the offence of which they are suspected and they are unwilling for these matters to be audio recorded, the suspect should be given the opportunity to tell the interviewer about these matters after the conclusion of the formal interview.

(E) Changing recording media

3.12   When the recorder shows the recording media only has a short time left to run, the interviewer shall so inform the person being interviewed and round off that part of the interview. If the interviewer leaves the room for a second set of recording media, the suspect shall not be left unattended. The interviewer will remove the recording media from the recorder and insert the new recording media which shall be unwrapped or opened in the suspect's presence. The recorder should be set to record on the new media. To avoid confusion between the recording media, the interviewer shall mark the media with an identification number immediately after it is removed from the recorder.

(F) Taking a break during interview

3.13   When a break is taken, the fact that a break is to be taken, the reason for it and the time shall be recorded on the audio recording.

3.14   When the break is taken and the interview room vacated by the suspect, the recording media shall be removed from the recorder and the procedures for the conclusion of an interview followed, see *paragraph 3.19*.

3.15   When a break is a short one and both the suspect and an interviewer remain in the interview room, the recording may be stopped. There is no need to remove the recording media and when the interview recommences the recording should continue on the same recording media. The time the interview recommences shall be recorded on the audio recording.

3.16   After any break in the interview the interviewer must, before resuming the interview, remind the person being questioned of their right to legal advice if they have not exercised it and that they remain under caution or, if there is any doubt, give the caution in full again. (See *Note 3G*.)

(G) Failure of recording equipment

3.17   If there is an equipment failure which can be rectified quickly, e.g. by inserting new recording media, the interviewer shall follow the appropriate procedures as in *paragraph 3.12*. When the recording is resumed the interviewer shall explain what happened and record the time the interview recommences. However, if it is not possible to continue recording using the same recording device or by using a replacement device, the interview should be audio-recorded using a secure digital recording network device as in *paragraph 4.1*, if the necessary equipment is available. If it is not available, the interview may continue and be recorded in writing in accordance with *paragraph 2.3* as directed by the 'relevant officer'. (See *Note 3H*.)

(H) Removing recording media from the recorder

3.18   Recording media which is removed from the recorder during the interview shall be retained and the procedures in *paragraph 3.12* followed.

(I) Conclusion of interview

3.19   At the conclusion of the interview, the suspect shall be offered the opportunity to clarify anything they have said and asked if there is anything they want to add.

3.20   At the conclusion of the interview, including the taking and reading back of any written statement, the time shall be recorded and the recording shall be stopped. The interviewer shall seal the master recording with a master recording label and treat it as an exhibit in accordance with force standing orders. The interviewer shall sign the label and ask the suspect and any third party present during the interview to sign it. If the suspect or third party refuse to sign the label an officer of at least the rank of inspector, or if not available the custody officer, or if the suspect has not been arrested, a sergeant, shall be called into the interview room and asked, subject to *paragraph 1.13*, to sign it.

3.21   The suspect shall be handed a notice which explains:

- how the audio recording will be used;
- the arrangements for access to it;
- that if they are charged or informed they will be prosecuted, a copy of the audio recording will be supplied as soon as practicable or as otherwise agreed between the suspect and the police or on the order of a court.

(J) After the interview

3.22   The interviewer shall make a note in their pocket book that the interview has taken place and that it was audibly recorded, the time it commenced, its duration and date and identification number of the master recording (see *Note 3I*).

3.23   If no proceedings follow in respect of the person whose interview was recorded, the recording media must be kept securely as in *paragraph 3.22* and *Note 3J*.

(K) Master Recording security

(i) General

3.24   The officer in charge of each police station at which interviews with suspects are recorded or as the case may be, where recordings of interviews carried out elsewhere than at a police station are held, shall make arrangements for master recordings to be kept securely and their movements accounted for on the same basis as material which may be used for evidential purposes, in accordance with force standing orders. (See *Note 3J*.)

(ii) Breaking master recording seal for criminal proceedings

3.25   A police officer has no authority to break the seal on a master recording which is required for criminal trial or appeal proceedings. If it is necessary to gain access to the master recording, the police officer shall arrange for its seal to be broken in the presence of a representative of the Crown Prosecution Service. The defendant or their legal adviser should be informed and given a reasonable opportunity to be present. If the defendant or their legal representative is present they shall be invited to re-seal and sign the master recording. If either refuses or neither is present this should be done by the representative of the Crown Prosecution Service. (See *Notes 3K and 3L*.)

(iii) Breaking master recording seal: other cases

3.26   The chief officer of police is responsible for establishing arrangements for breaking the seal of the master copy where no criminal proceedings result, or the criminal proceedings to which the interview relates, have been concluded and it becomes necessary to break the seal. These arrangements should be those which the chief officer considers are reasonably necessary to demonstrate to the person interviewed and any other party who may wish to use or refer to the interview record that the master copy has not been tampered with and that the interview record remains accurate. (See *Note 3M*.)

3.27   Subject to *paragraph 3.29*, a representative of each party must be given a reasonable opportunity to be present when the seal is broken and the master recording copied and re-sealed.

3.28   If one or more of the parties is not present when the master copy seal is broken because they cannot be contacted or refuse to attend or *paragraph 3.29* applies, arrangements should be made for an independent person such as a custody visitor, to be present. Alternatively, or as an additional safeguard, arrangements should be made to visually record the procedure.

3.29   *Paragraph 3.28* does not require a person to be given an opportunity to be present when;

- (a) it is necessary to break the master copy seal for the proper and effective further investigation of the original offence or the investigation of some other offence; and

(b) the officer in charge of the investigation has reasonable grounds to suspect that allowing an opportunity might prejudice such an investigation or criminal proceedings which may be brought as a result or endanger any person. (See *Note 3N*.)

(iv) Documentation

3.30   When the master recording seal is broken, a record must be made of the procedure followed, including the date, time, place and persons present.

Notes for guidance

Commencement of interviews (paragraph 3.3)

3A   *When outlining the recording process, the interviewer should refer to paragraph 1.6(a)(ii) and (iii) and briefly describe how the recording device being used is operated and how recordings are made. For the purpose of voice identification the interviewer should ask the suspect and any other people present to identify themselves.*

Interviews with suspects who appear to have a hearing impediment (paragraph 3.8)

3B   *This provision is to give a person who is deaf or has impaired hearing equivalent rights of access to the full interview record as far as this is possible using audio recording.*

3C   *The provisions of Code C on interpreters for suspects who do not appear to speak or understand English or who appear to have a hearing or speech impediment, continue to apply.*

Objections and complaints by the suspect (paragraph 3.9)

3D   *The relevant officer should be aware that a decision to continue recording against the wishes of the suspect may be the subject of comment in court.*

3E   *If the custody officer, or in the case of a person who has not been arrested, a sergeant, is called to deal with the complaint, the recorder should, if possible, be left on until the officer has entered the room and spoken to the person being interviewed. Continuation or termination of the interview should be at the interviewer's discretion pending action by an inspector under Code C, paragraph 9.2.*

3F   *If the complaint is about a matter not connected with this Code or Code C, the decision to continue is at the interviewer's discretion. When the interviewer decides to continue the interview, they shall tell the suspect that at the conclusion of the interview, the complaint will be brought to the attention of the custody officer, or in the case of a person who has not been arrested, a sergeant. When the interview is concluded the interviewer must, as soon as practicable, inform the custody officer or, as the case may be, the sergeant, about the existence and nature of the complaint made.*

3G   *In considering whether to caution again after a break, the interviewer should bear in mind that they may have to satisfy a court that the person understood that they were still under caution when the interview resumed. The interviewer should also remember that it may be necessary to show to the court that nothing occurred during a break or between interviews which influenced the suspect's recorded evidence. After a break or at the beginning of a subsequent interview, the interviewer should consider summarising on the record the reason for the break and confirming this with the suspect.*

Failure of recording equipment (paragraph 3.17)

3H   *Where the interview is being recorded and the media or the recording equipment fails the interviewer should stop the interview immediately. Where part of the interview is unaffected by the error and is still accessible on the media, that part shall be copied and sealed in the suspect's presence as a master copy and the interview recommenced using new equipment/media as required. Where the content of the interview has been lost in its entirety, the media should be sealed in the suspect's presence and the interview begun again. If the recording equipment cannot be fixed and no replacement is immediately available, subject to paragraph 2.3, the interview should be recorded in accordance with Code C, section 11.*

3I   *Any written record of an audio recorded interview should be made in accordance with current national guidelines for police officers, police staff and CPS prosecutors concerned with the preparation, processing and submission of prosecution files.*

Master Recording security (paragraphs 3.24 to 3.30)

3J   *This section is concerned with the security of the master recording sealed at the conclusion of the interview. Care must be taken of working copy recordings because their loss or destruction may lead unnecessarily to the need to access master recordings.*

Breaking master recording seal for criminal proceedings (paragraph 3.25)

3K   *If the master recording has been delivered to the crown court for their keeping after committal for trial the crown prosecutor will apply to the chief clerk of the crown court centre for the release of the recording for unsealing by the crown prosecutor.*

3L   *Reference to the Crown Prosecution Service or to the crown prosecutor in this part of the Code should be taken to include any other body or person with a statutory responsibility for the proceedings for which the police recorded interview is required.*

Breaking master recording seal: other cases (paragraphs 3.26 to 3.29)

3M   *The most common reasons for needing access to master copies that are not required for criminal proceedings arise from civil actions and complaints against police and civil actions between individuals arising out of allegations of crime investigated by police.*

3N   *Paragraph 3.29(b) could apply, for example, when one or more of the outcomes or likely outcomes of the investigation might be; (i) the prosecution of one or more of the original suspects; (ii) the prosecution of someone previously not suspected, including someone who was originally a witness, and (iii) any original suspect being treated as a prosecution witness and when premature disclosure of any police action, particularly through contact with any parties involved, could lead to a real risk of compromising the investigation and endangering witnesses.*

4   Interview recording using secure digital recording network device.

(A) General

4.1   An authorised secure digital recording network device (see *paragraph 1.6(a)(iii)* does not use removable media and this section specifies the provisions which will apply when such a device is used. For ease of reference, it repeats in full some of the provisions of section 3 that apply to both types of recording device.

(B) Commencement of interviews

4.2   When the suspect is brought into the interview room or arrives at the location where the interview is to take place, the interviewer shall without delay and in the sight of the suspect, switch on the recording equipment and in accordance with the manufacturer's instructions start recording.

4.3   The interviewer must point out the sign or indicator which shows that the recording equipment is activated and is recording (see *paragraph 1.6(a)(iii)*) and shall then:

    (a) tell the suspect that the interview is being audibly recorded using an authorised *secure digital recording network device* and outline the recording process (see *Note 3A*);

    (b) subject to *paragraph 1.13*, give their name and rank and that of any other interviewer present;

    (c) ask the suspect and any other party present, e.g. the appropriate adult, a solicitor or interpreter, to identify themselves (see *Note 3A*);

    (d) state the date, time of commencement and place of the interview; and

    (e) inform the person that:

        • they will be given access to the recording of the interview in the event that they are charged or informed that they will be prosecuted but if they are not charged or informed that they will be prosecuted they will only be given access as agreed with the police or on the order of a court; and

- they will be given a written notice at the end of the interview setting out their rights to access the recording and what will happen to the recording.

(f) If equipment for remote monitoring of interviews as described in *paragraph 2.6* is installed, explain the contents of the notice to the suspect, solicitor and appropriate adult as required by *paragraph 2.6(d)* and point out the light that illuminates automatically as soon as remote monitoring is activated.

4.4   *Paragraphs 3.5* to *3.7* apply.

(C) Interviews with suspects who appear to have a hearing impediment

4.5   *Paragraph 3.8* applies.

(D) Objections and complaints by the suspect

4.6   *Paragraphs 3.9*, *3.10* and *3.11* apply.

(E) Taking a break during interview

4.7   When a break is taken, the fact that a break is to be taken, the reason for it and the time shall be recorded on the audio recording. The recording shall be stopped and the procedures in *paragraphs 4.11* and *4.12* for the conclusion of interview followed.

4.8   When the interview recommences the procedures in *paragraphs 4.2* to *4.3* for commencing an interview shall be followed to create a new file to record the continuation of the interview. The time the interview recommences shall be recorded on the audio recording.

4.9   After any break in the interview the interviewer must, before resuming the interview, remind the person being questioned of their right to legal advice if they have not exercised it and that they remain under caution or, if there is any doubt, give the caution in full again (see *Note 3G*).

(F) Failure of recording equipment

4.10   If there is an equipment failure which can be rectified quickly, e.g. by commencing a new secure digital network recording using the same device or a replacement device, the interviewer shall follow the appropriate procedures as in *paragraphs 4.7 to 4.9* *(Taking a break during interview)*. When the recording is resumed, the interviewer shall explain what happened and record the time the interview recommences. However, if it is not possible to continue recording on the same device or by using a replacement device, the interview should be audio-recorded on removable media as in *paragraph 3.3*, if the necessary equipment is available. If it is not available, the interview may continue and be recorded in writing in accordance with *paragraph 2.3* as directed by the 'relevant officer'. (See *Note 3H*.)

(G) Conclusion of interview

4.11   At the conclusion of the interview, the suspect shall be offered the opportunity to clarify anything he or she has said and asked if there is anything they want to add.

4.12   At the conclusion of the interview, including the taking and reading back of any written statement:

(a) the time shall be orally recorded.

(b) the suspect shall be handed a notice (see *Note 4A)* which explains:

- how the audio recording will be used

- the arrangements for access to it

- that if they are charged or informed that they will be prosecuted, they will be given access to the recording of the interview either electronically or by being given a copy on removable recording media, but if they are not charged or informed that they will prosecuted, they will only be given access as agreed with the police or on the order of a court.

(c) the suspect must be asked to confirm that he or she has received a copy of the notice at *sub-paragraph (b)* above. If the suspect fails to accept or to acknowledge receipt of the notice, the interviewer will state for the recording that a copy of the notice has been provided to the suspect and that he or she has refused to take a copy of the notice or has refused to acknowledge receipt.

(d) the time shall be recorded and the interviewer shall ensure that the interview record is saved to the device in the presence of the suspect and any third party present during the interview and notify them accordingly. The interviewer must then explain that the record will be transferred securely to the remote secure network file server (see *paragraph 4.15*). If the equipment is available to enable the record to be transferred there and then in the suspect's presence, then it should be so transferred. If it is transferred at a later time, the time and place of the transfer must be recorded. The suspect should then be informed that the interview is terminated.

(H) After the interview

4.13   The interviewer shall make a note in their pocket book that the interview has taken place and that it was audibly recorded, time it commenced, its duration and date and the identification number, filename or other reference for the recording (see *Note 3I*).

4.14   If no proceedings follow in respect of the person whose interview was recorded, the recordings must be kept securely as in *paragraphs 4.15* and *4.16*.

(I) Security of secure digital network interview records

4.15   The recordings are first saved locally on the device before being transferred to the remote network file server system (see *paragraph 1.6(a)(iii)*). The recording remains on the local device until the transfer is complete. If for any reason the network connection fails, the recording will be transferred when the network connection is restored (see *paragraph 4.12(d)*). The interview record files are stored in read only form on non-removable storage devices, for example, hard disk drives, to ensure their integrity.

4.16   Access to interview recordings, including copying to removable media, must be strictly controlled and monitored to ensure that access is restricted to those who have been given specific permission to access for specified purposes when this is necessary. For example, police officers and CPS lawyers involved in the preparation of any prosecution case, persons interviewed if they have been charged or informed they may be prosecuted and their legal representatives.

Note for Guidance

4A   The notice at paragraph 4.12(b) above should provide a brief explanation of the secure digital network and how access to the recording is strictly limited. The notice should also explain the access rights of the suspect, their legal representative, the police and the prosecutor to the recording of the interview. Space should be provided on the form to insert the date, the identification number, filename or other reference for the interview recording.

ANNEX: PARAGRAPH 2.4(c)(iii) – FOUR INDICTABLE OFFENCE TYPES FOR WHICH THE INTERVIEWER MAY DECIDE TO MAKE A WRITTEN RECORD OF A VOLUNTARY INTERVIEW ELSEWHERE THAN AT A POLICE STATION WHEN AN AUTHORISED AUDIO RECORDING DEVICE CANNOT BE USED.

[See *Notes 2* and *3*]

Part 1: Four specified indictable offence types – two conditions

1. The **first** condition is that the *indictable* offence in respect of which the person has been cautioned is *one* of the following:

    (a) Possession of a controlled drug contrary to section 5(2) of the Misuse of Drugs Act 1971 if the drug is cannabis as defined by that Act and in a form commonly known as herbal cannabis or cannabis resin (see *Note 5*);

    (b) Possession of a controlled drug contrary to section 5(2) of the Misuse of Drugs Act 1971 if the drug is khat as defined by that Act (see *Note 5*);

    (c) Retail theft (shoplifting) contrary to section 1 of the Theft Act 1968 (see *Note 6*); and

    (d) Criminal damage to property contrary to section 1(1) of the Criminal Damage Act 1971 (see *Note 6*),

    and in this paragraph, the reference to each of the above offences applies to an attempt to commit that offence as defined by section 1 of the Criminal Attempts Act 1981.

2. The **second** condition is that:

    (a) where the person has been cautioned in respect of an offence described in *paragraph 1(a)* (Possession of herbal cannabis or cannabis resin) or *paragraph 1(b)* (Possession of khat), the requirements of *paragraphs 3 and 4* are satisfied; or

    (b) where the person has been cautioned in respect of an offence described in *paragraph 1(c)* (Retail theft), the requirements of *paragraphs 3 and 5* are satisfied; or

    (c) where the person has been cautioned in respect of an offence described in *paragraph 1(d)* (criminal damage), the requirements of *paragraphs 3 and 6* are satisfied.

3. The requirements of this paragraph that apply to all four offences described in *paragraph 1* are that:

    (i) with regard to the person suspected of committing the offence:

    - they appear to be aged 18 or over;

    - there is no reason to suspect that they are a vulnerable person for whom an appropriate adult is required (see *paragraph 1.5* of this Code);

    - they do *not* appear to be unable to understand what is happening because of the effects of drink, drugs or illness, ailment or condition;

    - they do *not* require an interpreter in accordance with *Code C section 13*; and

    - in accordance with Code G (Arrest), their arrest is *not* necessary in order to investigate the offence;

    (ii) it appears that the commission of the offence:

    - has *not* resulted in any injury to any person;

    - has *not* involved any realistic threat or risk of injury to any person; and

    - has *not* caused any *substantial* financial or material loss to the private property of any individual; and

    (iii) the person is not being interviewed about any other offence.

    See *Notes 3* and *8*.

4. The requirements of this paragraph that apply to the offences described in *paragraph 1(a)* (possession of herbal cannabis or cannabis resin) and *paragraph 1(b)* (possession of khat) are that a police officer who is experienced in the recognition of the physical appearance, texture and smell of herbal cannabis, cannabis resin or (as the case may be) khat, is able to say that the substance which has been found in the suspect's possession by that officer or, as the case may be, by any other officer not so experienced and trained:

    (i)   is a controlled drug being either herbal cannabis, cannabis resin or khat; and

    (ii) the quantity of the substance found is consistent with personal use by the suspect and does not provide any grounds to suspect an intention to supply others.

    See *Note 5*.

5. The requirements of this paragraph that apply to the offence described in *paragraph 1(c)* (retail theft), are that it appears to the officer:

    (i)   that the value of the property stolen does not exceed £100 inclusive of VAT;

    (ii) that the stolen property has been recovered and remains fit for sale unless the items stolen comprised drink or food and have been consumed; and

    (iii) that the person suspected of stealing the property is not employed (whether paid or not) by the person, company or organisation to which the property belongs.

    See *Note 3*.

6. The requirements of this paragraph that apply to the offence described in *paragraph 1(d)* (Criminal damage), are that it appears to the officer:

    (i)   that the value of the criminal damage does *not exceed* £300; and

    (ii) that the person suspected of damaging the property is not employed (whether paid or not) by the person, company or organisation to which the property belongs.

    See *Note 3*.

Part 2: Other provisions applicable to all interviews to which this Annex applies

7. *Paragraphs 3.21 to 3.22B of Code C set out the responsibilities of the interviewing officer for ensuring compliance with the provisions of Code C that apply to the conduct and recording of voluntary interviews to which this Annex applies. See Note 7.*

8. If it appears to the interviewing officer that before the conclusion of an interview, any of the requirements in *paragraphs 3 to 6 of Part 1* that apply to the offence in question described in *paragraph 1* of Part 1 have ceased to apply; this Annex shall cease to apply. The person being interviewed must be so informed and a break in the interview must be taken. The reason must be recorded in the written interview record and the continuation of the interview shall be audio recorded in accordance with *section 2 of this Code*. For the purpose of the continuation, the provisions of *paragraphs 3.3* and *4.2* (Commencement of interviews) shall apply. See *Note 8*.

Notes for Guidance

1. *Not used.*

2. *The purpose of allowing the interviewer to decide that a written record is to be made is to support the policy which gives police in England and Wales options for dealing with low-level offences quickly and non-bureaucratically in a proportionate manner. Guidance for police about these options is available at:*

    https://www.app.college.police.uk/app-content/prosecution-and-case-management/justice-outcomes/.

3   *A decision in relation to a particular indictable offence that the conditions and requirements in this Annex are satisfied is an operational matter for the interviewing officer according to all the particular circumstances of the case. These circumstances include the outcome of the officer's investigation at that time and any other matters that are relevant to the officer's consideration as to how to deal with the matter.*

4   *Not used.*

5   *Under the Misuse of Drugs Act 1971 as at the date this Code comes into force:*

    (a)   *cannabis includes any part of the cannabis plant but not mature stalks and seeds separated from the plant, cannabis resin and cannabis oil, but paragraph 1(a) applies only to the possession of herbal cannabis and cannabis resin; and*

    (b)   *khat includes the leaves, stems and shoots of the plant.*

6   *The power to issue a Penalty Notice for Disorder (PND) for an offence contrary to section 1 of the Theft Act 1968 applies when the value of the goods stolen does not exceed £100 inclusive of VAT. The power to issue a PND for an offence contrary to section 1(1) of the Criminal Damage Act 1971 applies when the value of the damage does not exceed £300.*

7   *The provisions of Code C that apply to the conduct and recording of voluntary interviews to which this Annex applies are described in paragraphs 3.21 to 3.22B of Code C. They include the suspect's right to free legal advice, the provision of information about the offence before the interview (see Code C paragraph 11.1A) and the right to interpretation and translation (see Code C section 13). These and other rights and entitlements are summarised in the notice that must be given to the suspect.*

8   *The requirements in paragraph 3 of Part 1 will cease to apply if, for example during the course of an interview, as a result of what the suspect says or other information which comes to the interviewing officer's notice:*

- *it appears that the suspect:*
    - *is aged under 18;*
    - *does require an appropriate adult;*
    - *is unable to appreciate the significance of questions and their answers;*
    - *is unable to understand what is happening because of the effects of drink, drugs or illness, ailment or condition; or*
    - *requires an interpreter; or*
- *the police officer decides that the suspect's arrest is now necessary (see Code G).*

POLICE AND CRIMINAL EVIDENCE ACT 1984 (PACE)

CODE F

REVISED

CODE OF PRACTICE ON VISUAL RECORDING WITH SOUND OF INTERVIEWS WITH SUSPECTS

Commencement - Transitional Arrangements

This contents of this Code should be considered if an interviewer proposes to make a visual recording with sound of an interview with a suspect after 00.00 on 31 July 2018.

There is no statutory requirement under PACE to visually record interviews.

Code F - Contents

1   General

1.0   The procedures in this Code must be used fairly, responsibly, with respect for the people to whom they apply and without unlawful discrimination. Under the Equality Act 2010, section 149 (Public Sector Equality Duty), police forces must, in carrying out their functions, have due regard to the need to eliminate unlawful discrimination, harassment, victimisation and any other conduct which is prohibited by that Act, to advance equality of opportunity between people who share a relevant protected characteristic and people who do not share it, and to foster good relations between those persons. The Equality Act *also* makes it unlawful for police officers to discriminate against, harass or victimise any person on the grounds of the 'protected characteristics' of age, disability, gender reassignment, race, religion or belief, sex and sexual orientation, marriage and civil partnership, pregnancy and maternity, when using their powers. See *Note 1C*.

1.1   This Code of Practice must be readily available for consultation by police officers and other police staff, detained persons and members of the public.

1.2   The *Notes for Guidance* included are not provisions of this code. They form guidance to police officers and others about its application and interpretation.

1.3   Nothing in this Code shall detract from the requirements of Code C, the Code of Practice for the detention, treatment and questioning of persons by police officers.

1.4   The interviews and matters to which this Code applies and provisions that govern the conduct and recording of those interviews and other matters are described in section 2.

   Note: The provisions of this Code and Code E which govern the conduct and recording of interviews *do not apply* to interviews with, or taking statements from, witnesses.

1.5   *Not used.*

1.5A   The provisions of Code E which require interviews with suspects to be audio recorded and the provisions of this Code which permit simultaneous visual recording provide safeguards:

- for suspects against inaccurate recording of the words used in questioning them and of their demeanour during the interview; and

- for police interviewers against unfounded allegations made by, or on behalf of, suspects about the conduct of the interview and what took place during the interview which might otherwise appear credible.

   The visual recording of interviews must therefore be carried out openly to instil confidence in its reliability as an impartial and accurate record of the interview.

1.6   *Not used.*

1.6A   *Not used.*

1.7   *Not used.*

1.8   *Not used.*

Notes for Guidance

1A   Not used.

1B   Not used.

1C   In paragraph 1.0, under the Equality Act 2010, section 149, the 'relevant protected characteristics' are: age, disability, gender reassignment, pregnancy and maternity, race, religion/belief, and sex and sexual orientation. For further detailed guidance and advice on the Equality Act, see: https://www.gov.uk/guidance/equality-act-2010-guidance.

2.   When interviews and matters to which Code F applies may be visually recorded with sound and provisions for their conduct and recording.

(A) General

2.1   For the purpose of this Code, a visual recording with sound means an audio recording of an interview or other matter made in accordance with the requirement in *paragraph 2.1* of the Code of Practice on audio recording interviews with suspects (Code E) (see *Note 2A*) during which a *simultaneous* visual recording is made which shows the suspect, the interviewer and those in whose presence and hearing the audio recording was made.

2.2   There is no statutory requirement to make a visual recording, however, the provisions of this Code shall be followed on any occasion that the 'relevant officer' described in *Code E paragraph 2.4* considers that a visual recording of any matters mentioned in *paragraph 2.1* should be made. Having regard to the safeguards described in *paragraph 1.5A*, examples of occasions when the relevant officer is likely to consider that a visual recording should be made include when:

(a)   the suspect (whether or not detained) requires an appropriate adult;

(b)   the suspect or their solicitor or appropriate adult requests that the interview be recorded visually;

(c)   the suspect or other person whose presence is necessary is deaf or deaf/blind or speech impaired and uses sign language to communicate;

(d)   the interviewer anticipates that when asking the suspect about their involvement in the offence concerned, they will invite the suspect to demonstrate their actions or behaviour at the time or to examine a particular item or object which is handed to them;

(e)   the officer in charge of the investigation believes that a visual recording with sound will assist in the conduct of the investigation, for example, when briefing other officers about the suspect or matters coming to light during the course of the interview; and

(f)   the authorised recording device that would be used in accordance with *paragraph 2.1 of Code E* incorporates a camera and creates a combined audio and visual recording and does not allow the visual recording function to operate independently of the audio recording function.

2.3   For the purpose of making such a visual recording, the provisions of Code E and the relevant *Notes for Guidance* shall apply equally to visual recordings with sound as they do to audio-only recordings, subject to the additional provisions in *paragraphs 2.5 to 2.12* below which apply exclusively to visual recordings. (See *Note 2E*.)

2.4   This Code does not apply to the conduct and recording in England and Wales, of:

- interviews of persons detained under section 41 of, or Schedule 7 to, the Terrorism Act 2000, and
- post-charge questioning of persons authorised under section 22 of the Counter-Terrorism Act 2008.

These must be video recorded with sound in accordance with the provisions of the separate Code of Practice issued under paragraph 3 of Schedule 8 to the Terrorism Act 2000 and under section 25 of the Counter-Terrorism Act 2008. If, during the course of an interview or questioning being visually recorded under this Code, it becomes apparent that the interview or questioning should be conducted under that separate Code, the interview should only continue in accordance with that Code (see *Code E paragraph 1.4*).

(B) Application of <u>Code E</u> – additional provisions that apply to visual recording with sound.

(i) General

2.5   Before visual recording commences, the interviewer must inform the suspect that in accordance with *paragraph 2.2*, a visual recording is being made and explain the visual and audio recording arrangements. If the suspect is a juvenile or a vulnerable person (see Code C, *paragraphs 1.4, 1.5* and *1.13(d)*), the information and explanation must be provided or (as the case may be) provided again, in the presence of the appropriate adult.

2.6   The device used to make the visual recording at the same time as the audio recording (see *paragraph 2.1*) must ensure coverage of as much of the room or location where the interview takes place as it is practically possible to achieve whilst the interview takes place (see *Note 2B*).

2.7   In cases to which *paragraph 1.13 of Code E* (disclosure of identity of officers or police staff conducting interviews) applies:

(a)   the officers and staff may have their backs to the visual recording device; and

(b)   when in accordance with <u>Code E paragraph 3.21</u> or *4.12* as they apply to this Code, arrangements are made for the suspect to have access to the visual recording, the investigating officer may arrange for anything in the recording that might allow the officers or police staff to be identified to be concealed.

2.8   Following a decision made by the relevant officer in accordance with *paragraph 2.2* that an interview or other matter mentioned in *paragraph 2.1* above should be *visually recorded*, the relevant officer may decide that the interview is not to be visually recorded if it no longer appears that a visual recording should be made or because of a fault in the recording device. However, a decision not to make a *visual recording* does not detract in any way from the requirement for the interview to be *audio recorded* in accordance with *paragraph 2.1 of Code E*. (See *Note 2C*.)

2.9   The provisions in <u>Code E paragraph 2.6</u> for remote monitoring of interviews shall apply to visually recorded interviews.

(ii) Objections and complaints by the suspect about visual recording

2.10   If the suspect or an appropriate adult on their behalf objects to the interview being *visually* recorded either at the outset or during the interview or during a break in the interview, the interviewer shall explain that the visual recording is being made in accordance with *paragraph 2.2* and that this Code requires the objections to be recorded on the *visual* recording. When any objections have been recorded or the suspect or the appropriate adult have refused to have their objections recorded visually, the relevant officer shall decide in accordance with *paragraph 2.8* and having regard to the nature and circumstances of the objections, whether visual recording should be turned off (see *Note 2D*). Following a decision that visual recording should be turned off, the interviewer shall say that they are turning off the *visual* recording. The audio recording required to be maintained in accordance with <u>Code E</u> shall continue and the interviewer shall ask the person to record their objections to the interview being *visually* recorded on the audio recording. If the relevant officer considers that visual recording should not be turned off, the interviewer may proceed to question the suspect with the visual recording still on. If the suspect also objects to the interview being audio recorded, *paragraph 3.9 of Code E* will apply if a removable recording media device (see <u>Code E paragraph 1.6(a)(ii)</u>) is being used) and *paragraph 4.6 of Code E* will apply if a secure digital recording device (see <u>Code E paragraph 1.6(a)(iii)</u>) is being used.

2.11   If the suspect indicates that they wish to tell the interviewer about matters not directly connected with the offence of which they are suspected and that they are unwilling for these matters to be visually recorded, the suspect should be given the opportunity to tell the interviewer about these matters after the conclusion of the formal interview.

(ii) Failure of visual recording device

2.12   If there is a failure of equipment and it is not possible to continue visual recording using the same type of recording device (i.e. a removable recording media device as in Code E *paragraph 1.6(a)(ii)* or a secure digital recording network device as in Code E *paragraph 1.6(a)(iii)*) or by using a replacement device of either type, the relevant officer may decide that the interview is to continue without being visually recorded. In these circumstances, the continuation of the interview must be conducted and recorded in accordance with the provisions of Code E (See *Note 2F.*)

Notes for Guidance

2A   *Paragraph 2.1 of Code E describes the requirement that authorised audio-recording devices are to be used for recording interviews and other matters.*

2B   *Interviewers will wish to arrange that, as far as possible, visual recording arrangements are unobtrusive. It must be clear to the suspect, however, that there is no opportunity to interfere with the recording equipment or the recording media.*

2C   *A decision made in accordance with paragraph 2.8 not to record an interview visually for any reason may be the subject of comment in court. The 'relevant officer' responsible should therefore be prepared to justify that decision.*

2D   *Objections for the purpose of paragraph 2.10 are meant to apply to objections based on the suspect's genuine and honestly held beliefs and to allow officers to exercise their discretion to decide whether a visual recording is to be made according to the circumstances surrounding the suspect and the investigation. Objections that appear to be frivolous with the intentions of frustrating or delaying the investigation would not be relevant.*

2E   *The visual recording made in accordance with this Code may be used for eye-witness identification procedures to which paragraph 3.21 and Annex E of Code D apply.*

2F   *Where the interview is being visually recorded and the media or the recording device fails, the interviewer should stop the interview immediately. Where part of the interview is unaffected by the error and is still accessible on the media or on the network device, that part shall be copied and sealed in the suspect's presence as a master copy or saved as a new secure digital network recording as appropriate. The interview should then be recommenced using a functioning recording device and new recording media as appropriate. Where the media content of the interview has been lost in its entirety, the media should be sealed in the suspect's presence and the interview begun again. If the visual recording equipment cannot be fixed and a replacement device is not immediately available, the interview should be audio recorded in accordance with Code E.*

2G   *The relevant officer should be aware that a decision to continue visual recording against the wishes of the suspect may be the subject of comment in court.*

Adapted and published by GRANGIS under the OGL Licence.
GRANGIS - UK PUBLISHING 2022.
Thank you for taking the time to leave us a review regarding this edition"

For further inquiries, please feel free to contact us at:
www.grangis.com / contact@grangis.com

www.ingramcontent.com/pod-product-compliance
Lightning Source LLC
Chambersburg PA
CBHW072143150726
48002CB00004B/1603